ideals®

MOTHER'S DAY

D0478252

Vol. 48, No. 3

Publisher, Patricia A. Pingry
Editor, Nancy J. Skarmeas
Editorial Assistant, LaNita Kirby
Art Director, Patrick McRae

ISBN 0-8249-1090-7

IDEALS—Vol. 48, No. 3 May MCMXCI IDEALS (ISSN 0019-137X) is published eight times a year: February, March, May, June, August, September, November, December by IDEALS PUBLISHING CORPORATION, P.O. Box 148000, Nashville, Tenn. 37214. Second-class postage paid at Nashville, Tennessee, and additional mailing offices. Copyright © MCMXCI by IDEALS PUBLISHING CORPORATION. POSTMASTER: Send address changes to Ideals, Post Office Box 148000, Nashville, Tenn. 37214-8000. All rights reserved. Title IDEALS registered U.S. Patent Office.

SINGLE ISSUE—$4.95
ONE-YEAR SUBSCRIPTION—eight consecutive issues as published—$19.95
TWO-YEAR SUBSCRIPTION—sixteen consecutive issues as published—$35.95
Outside U.S.A., add $6.00 per subscription year for postage and handling.

ACKNOWLEDGMENTS

WISE MOTHERS from *FLAME IN THE WIND* by Grace Noll Crowell. Copyright © 1939, 1958 by Grace Noll Crowell. Reprinted by permission of HarperCollins Publishers; MOTHER LOVE used by permission of Katherine Edelman Lyon, Literary Executrix for Katherine Edelman; MOTHER'S WAY by Edgar A. Guest. Used by permission of the estate; SPRING GARDEN by Vera Laurel Hoffman. Used by permission of the estate; SPRING . . . MAKER OF DREAMS from *THE SOARING FLAME*, copyright 1948 by Mary O'Connor. Used by permission. A SOWER'S PRAYER by Ruth Gibbs Zwall from *HILLS OF GOD*, first published in *CHRISTIAN HERALD*. Used by permission. MAY EVER LIVES by Edgar Daniel Kramer. Used by permission of the estate. SYNONYMOUS from *HARBOR HUNGER* by Bettie Payne Welles. Used by permission of the estate. THE WEAVER, MAY by Stella Craft Tremble. Used by permission of the estate. Our sincere thanks to the following whose addresses we have been unable to locate: Joy Belle Burgess for A MOTHER'S LOVE; Alice B. Johnson for A MOTHER'S HEART; Marion Plunkett for PORTRAIT; Goldie Capers Smith for MY MOTHER WALKED BY NIGHT; Jeannette Stone for SPRING'S MORNING LIGHT; Lucille Key Thompson for INFORMAL GARDEN; Charles L. H. Wagner for THE PERFECT WORD; Milly Walton for LILACS; Jean Warren for TO MY MOTHER; Vera Hardman for IN BEAUTY.

Four-color separations by Rayson Films, Inc., Waukesha, Wisconsin

Printing by The Banta Company, Menasha, Wisconsin

The paper used in this publication meets the minimum requirements of American National Standard for Information Sciences—Permanence of Paper for Printed Library Materials, ANSI Z39.48-1984.

Unsolicited manuscripts will not be returned without a self-addressed stamped envelope.

Inside Front Cover   Inside Back Cover   Cover Photo
Frances Hook   Gerald Koser   Fred Sieb

Spring's Morning Light

Jeannette Stone

I looked into the beauty of the day
At all of nature born again on earth.
The peaceful light of spring's new morning lay
So pure and fresh in innocence of birth.
And I, within my heart, was singing songs
In spirit which can make one safe and whole
Where every human heart on earth belongs,
With spring's conversion of the winter soul.
I saw the joy and peace of spring anew
Like humble souls laid bare before their God
When pure white peace of love comes rushing through
Like mighty rain-washed floods upon the sod.
    There in the beauty of the awesome sight
    My soul was lifted up on wings of light.

Photo Opposite
MOUNTAIN LAUREL
Shenandoah National Park, Virginia
Johnson's Photography/Bill Johnson

Spring . . . Maker of Dreams

Mary O'Connor

She stains her youthful lips with wild strawberries,
Puts violets in her green and flowing hair;
She lays arbutus rugs beneath wild cherries
As trillium lanterns quiver in the air.

She dares the shadow's gloom to curb the spirit,
And turns despair to laughter's rainbow light;
Gloom can never thrive when she is near it
For she is promise rising out of night.

She puts her ivy arms around the hedges
And draws the world together hills and streams;
She trims away the tough and ragged edges
And fills mankind with tenderness and dreams.

Photo Opposite
CRABAPPLE IN BLOOM
Gene Ahrens/H. Armstrong Roberts

Photo Overleaf
VILLAGE VISTA
Ontario, Wisconsin
Ken Dequaine Photography

THE WEAVER, MAY

Stella Craft Tremble

The weaver, May, before her loom
Began to weave the weather:
For warp and woof she used sunbeams
And songs of birds together.

From out her weft fell drops of pearls
To spangle reeds and rushes;
And then she whisked some silver notes
For morning song of thrushes.

She added hanks of fleecy skies
All banked with crystal edges;
Threw bolts of yellow daisies down
To trim roadside hedges.

Her threads of iridescent light
Transformed the hill and heather;
May wound her shuttle with bouquets,
And loosed skeins of golden weather!

Photo Opposite
FOREST PARK, EVERETT, WASHINGTON
Ed Cooper Photography

LILACS
Gene Ahrens, Photographer

Lilacs

Milly Walton

Lilacs in the rain,
Silver mist in purple plumes,
The scent of clean-washed earth
Blends with their sweet perfume.

Lilacs in the dusk,
Ethereal in the pale moonlight,
Fragrance, like a wistful ghost,
Paints the beauty of the night.

Lilacs in the spring,
Ladies of old-fashioned grace,
Clinging to youthful memories
Of love, in lavender and lace.

BLUE VIOLET
Adam Jones, Photographer

The Violet

Jane Taylor

Down in a green and shady bed
   A modest violet grew;
Its stalk was bent, it hung its head,
   As if to hide from view.

And there it was content to bloom,
   In modest tints arrayed;
And there diffused a sweet perfume,
   Within the silent shade.

Then let me to the valley go,
   This pretty flower to see,
That I might also learn to grow
   In sweet humility.

Informal Garden

Lucile Key Thompson

My garden has a friendly air
   Of informality:

A fence and gate, a praying rock
   Beneath a dogwood tree,

Roses climbing trellises,
   Lilies serving wine

From slender cup of amethyst
   Beneath a smilax vine,

And flower beds as scatter rugs
   Upon the new green sod

Where all the tender leaves of grass
   Point to the face of God!

NANTUCKET ISLAND
Massachusetts
Barbara Laatsch-Hupp, Photographer

Spring Garden

Vera Laurel Hoffman

I have an hour I must keep
Close to the brown and fragrant earth,
To spade and hoe and dig and plant,
And know again this bright rebirth.

When sun is warm and spring is new,
And robins fill the day
With patches of their bright, red breasts
And songs along the way,

I have an hour I must spend
In pulling weeds and such,
In planting bulbs and tiny seeds
To feel the stirring touch

Of life upon the living soil:
The sun, the warmth, the sod.
Here in bright tranquility
I labor close to God.

Photo Opposite
HERB GARDEN
Marietta, Pennsylvania
Lefever/Grushow
Grant Heilman Photography, Inc.

ROSES AND FENCE, Dick Dietrich Photography

SYNONYMOUS

Bettie Payne Welles

I held a rosebud
in my hand
And watched each
petal unfold;

I marveled at
the beauty
And wonder
which it told.

PINK ROSE, Dick Dietrich Photography

In my arms
   I held a babe,
Treasure of
   the earth;
Tightly I clasped
   its form—
The miracle
   of birth.

The rose bud
   as the babe;
The babe
   as unblown rose:
Each will
   unfold glory
That heaven
   only knows.

FROM MY GARDEN JOURNAL

Deana Deck

The Color and Variety of the Iris

May brings the brilliant colors of the iris to gardens all across the country. This lovely flower, which takes its name from the Greek goddess of the rainbow, blooms in an almost overwhelming array of colors and is referred to by many gardeners simply as "the flag."

The native colors of the iris are limited mostly to lavenders, yellows, and white; but with these as a starting point, hybridizers have created a palette that includes bold reds, bronzes, a near-black, delicate creamy ivory, pale pink, and more. Each new color is a wonderful discovery. It is not infrequently that I find myself asking perfect strangers for a division from their plants. Fortunately, iris gardeners are usually more than willing to share their bounty.

Hundreds of exotic combinations have also been developed. There are bi-colors, which feature a standard (three upright petals) of one color and a fall (three lower petals) of another; bi-tones, which present contrasting shades of the same color; and blends, which display two colors gently shaded together in each petal.

Irises thrive in just about any climate and are native throughout the world, although they do best in northern temperate zones. A glance at the characteristics of some of the many iris varieties reveals that there is an iris for just about any climate, soil, or light situation.

In addition to the familiar bearded iris that graces so many older gardens, the two other species most popular with gardeners are the Japanese iris and the Siberian iris.

The Japanese iris, also known as the marsh iris, thrives beside ponds and in boggy soil. It is perfect for low-lying areas of the garden where drainage is a problem. This iris requires an acidic soil constantly kept moist.

The Siberian iris, as its name implies, is an exceptionally hardy type with narrow, grass-like leaves. This iris does very well in areas with extreme winters and slightly acidic, fairly moist soil. The Siberian is the parent species of many hybrids.

Most irises grow from rhizomes, but others grow from bulbs. The bulb varieties are a good choice for early spring blooming. For southern gardeners there is the Louisiana iris, which loves hot and humid summers. Unlike other varieties, it requires mulching to protect the rhizome.

In an area with moist, sandy soil and fairly mild winters, the Roof Iris is the species to seek. Native to China and Japan, this iris will remain evergreen if the temperature does not drop below twenty degrees.

If you enjoy patio or container gardening, there are even some dwarf varieties to try. The Crested Iris grows only four or five inches in height and produces diminutive lavender-blue flowers with yellow crests and a delicate fragrance. It likes the partial shade common to most balcony or patio gardens. If you keep the plant moist, however, it will also do well in full sun.

Irises are one of the easiest perennials to grow if you follow a few very basic guidelines. Do not plant them in the middle of the flower bed. Instead, isolate the iris at one edge, or better yet, give it a home of its own. The reason is that most perennials and annuals require frequent watering throughout the season, while most iris varieties require a drier soil after they have finished blooming. And do not mulch unless you have a specific species that requires it. Irises like to have the sun on their feet. They grow best when planted on a mound of soil, with the upper portion of the rhizome barely exposed at the surface. Beardless varieties need to be planted a little deeper and will require heavier feeding, more moisture, and a more acidic soil.

As with any perennial, a well-prepared bed will result in better growth and more blooms. Prepare the planting area by digging deeply and amending the soil with copious amounts of organic matter, compost, and manure. If the soil is heavy, mix in some sand to help promote drainage.

Bearded irises are best planted and divided in July and August, after going dormant. For a good showing the first year, plant three rhizomes together, each pointing inward to form a triangle. Beardless irises should be planted and divided in fall or spring and watered heavily when transplanted.

In general, feed most irises in early spring and again soon after blooming with a 6-12-12 fertilizer. Add superphosphate in fall by gently scratching it into the soil around the roots.

The iris's worst enemy is the iris borer, and prevention is the best control of this pest. In fall, clean up all debris around the plants, cut the foliage back at the base, and discard any that appears damaged by burning. Do not compost.

Iris foliage remains attractive long after blooming has ceased, and it makes for useful background plants. They are also suitable as ground cover in difficult-to-mow areas such as terraced banks, where they will hold soil and prevent erosion.

But most of all, the iris brings color to your garden. Whatever color flag you seek to unfurl, the iris—the rainbow flower—is likely your best bet.

Deana Deck lives in Nashville, Tennessee, where her garden column is a regular feature in the Tennessean.

A Sower's Prayer

Ruth Gibbs Zwall

God of all gardens
　　and growing things,
Of quickened seeds
　　and strong, bright wings,
Here are my hands
　　that fumble so:
Teach them how
　　to plant and grow.
Use them to make
　　a furrow straight,
Counting no task
　　too small, too great
If from the ground
　　someone will see
A radiant flower
　　bloom for Thee.

God of all homes
　　and houses where
Faith has an altar
　　reared for prayer,
Here are my lips
　　that stumble so:
Teach them to help
　　a child grow.
Give them patience
　　and truth to guide
Little steps
　　to your side,
That in the harvest
　　there may be
A child, a youth,
　　a life for Thee.

GARDEN AT CHARLES DEMUTH FOUNDATION
Lancaster, Pennsylvania
Lefever/Grushow
Grant Heilman Photography, Inc.

Thoughts of a Busy Mother

Katherine Cahill

If I can't find the time to wash the floor,
Who will remember or care?
If I don't patch the hole in their blue jeans,
They can wear another pair.

The dust can sit right where it is,
For tomorrow there will be more.
If the day is too short to bake a cake,
I can always run to the store.

But if I forget to wipe a tear
Or to kiss an injured knee,
To cheer a frown, turn it upside down
Until they're chuckling with glee;

If I would fail to stop and chat
When their tales are filled with woe,
To listen for unspoken words
That only sad eyes show;

If I missed a chance to see the world
Through their precious eyes . . .
A dandelion, a crawly bug,
A rainbow in the sky . . .

Then I've missed a chance to share the day
With one I hold most dear;
For God was knocking at my heart
And I was too busy to hear.

THE PERFECT WORD

Charles L. H. Wagner

The word defining home and peace,
The word implying grace;
Symbolic of divinity,
And angel's smiling face.
The word that is a synonym
For sacrifice supreme,
For kindliness and charity,
For love that can redeem.
The word for tender caring,
For hope that cheers the heart,
The perfect word
That makes the world
Seem heaven's counterpart:
Mother.

Photo Opposite
VICTORIAN FARMSTEAD
Leland, Wisconsin
Ken Dequaine Photography

BITS & PIECES

Nothing can compare in beauty, and wonder, and admirableness, and divinity itself, to the silent work in obscure dwellings of faithful women bringing their children to honor and virtue and piety.

Henry Ward Beecher

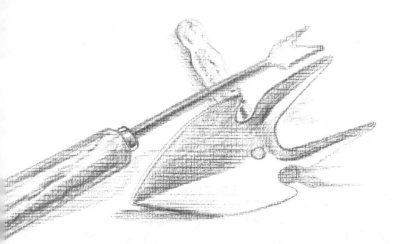

The angels, whispering to one another, can find, among their burning terms of love, none so devotional as that of "Mother."

Edgar Allan Poe

Most of all the beautiful things in life come by twos and threes, by dozens and hundreds. Plenty of roses, stars, sunsets, rainbows, brothers and sisters, aunts and cousins, but only one mother in the whole world.

Kate Douglas Wiggin

No man is poor who has a godly mother.

Abraham Lincoln

Whereas the service rendered the United States by the American mother is the greatest source of the country's strength and admiration; and Whereas we honor ourselves and the mothers of America when we do any thing to give emphasis to the home as the fountainhead of the State; and Whereas the American mother is doing so much for good government and humanity, we declare that the second Sunday of May will henceforth be celebrated as Mother's Day.

Congressional Resolution, 1914

No language can express the power and beauty and heroism and majesty of a mother's love. It shrinks not where man cowers, and grows stronger where man faints, and over the wastes of worldly fortune sends the radiance of its quenchless fidelity like a star in heaven.

Edwin H. Chapin

MAY EVER LIVES

Edgar Daniel Kramer

May ever lives where baby feet
Run stumbling down the garden walk,
Where flowers lift their faces sweet
To harken to a baby's talk.

May ever lives where baby lips
Cling to my mouth in soft caress,
Where trembling rosebud fingertips
Thrill me with their loveliness.

May ever lives where baby's eyes,
Far fairer than the stars that gleam,
Lead me away to paradise
Along the paths of dew and dream.

Photo Opposite
SPRING TREE
Vermont
A. Griffin/H. Armstrong Roberts

NO THORNS

Lola Boone

I picked a pretty rose today
Then slowly tore each thorn away;
To spare my child the pricking hurt,
I threw them back into the dirt.
"And now it's perfect," so I thought.
Then I remembered I'd been taught
That thorns are there to let us know
That life's hard places make us grow.
We cannot spare each prick of pain,
As we can't take away the rain.
It's all part of the master plan.
Each one must learn with his own hand
That life is beautiful, yet should
Contain some bad things with the good
   That we may know reality.
   Perfection's for eternity.

GOOD MOTHER

Gail Brook Burket

Her love is like a tree which proffers shade
To all, yet never stifles lives with bounds.
Her children walk serenely unafraid,
Because they sense her glowing love confounds
The perils which encompass them, as light
Dispels the dark. Love in her trusting glance
Helps them to shun the wrong and choose the right.

Her love, like loaves, gives them rich sustenance
And cheers their hearts as fires warm chill rooms.
Like sunlight falling on a clover field,
Her love is golden-rayed and brings the blooms
To full perfection and abundant yield.
Her love is shining prophecy to show
Celestial love the hosts of heaven know.

A Mother's Gift

Virginia Larson

Once in my day of busy hours
You picked a small bouquet of flowers;
You came running in from frolic and play
To give me sunshine on a summer's day.

You picked them by the babbling brook
That sings along its way,
Then hurried home to Mother
With your sweet, golden bouquet.

Browned by the sun and tousle-haired
You showed your mother how you cared.
And I—among my busy hours—
Kissed the hand that held the flowers.

Little barefoot boy with cheeks of tan,
When you grow to be a man
I'll still remember the little flowers
That brightened my day of busy hours.

You gave me golden flowers
Made by God above,
But you gave me more than flowers, son,
You gave your mother love.

A SLICE OF LIFE

——— Edgar A. Guest ———

Mother's Way

Tender, gentle, brave and true,
Loving us whate'er we do!
Waiting, watching at the gate
For the footsteps that are late,
Sleepless through the hours of night
Till she knows that we're all right;
Pleased with every word we say—
That is every mother's way.

Others sneer and turn aside.
Mother welcomes us with pride;
Over-boastful of us, too,
Glorying in all we do,
First to praise and last to blame,
Love that always stays the same,
Following us where'er we stray—
That is every mother's way.

She would grant us all we seek,
Give her strength when we are weak.
Beauty? She would let it go
For the joy we yearn to know.
Life? She'd give it gladly, too,
For the dream that we pursue;
She would toil that we might play—
That is every mother's way.

Not enough for her are flowers—
Her life is so blent with ours
That in all we dare and do
She is partner, through and through;
Suffering when we suffer pain,
Happy when we smile again,
Living with us, night and day—
That is every mother's way.

*Edgar A. Guest began his career in 1895 at the age
of fourteen when his work first appeared in the*
Detroit Free Press. *His column was syndicated in
over 300 newspapers, and he became known as
"The Poet of the People."*

Nest Eggs

Robert Louis Stevenson

Birds all the sunny day
　Flutter and quarrel
Here in the arbor-like
　Tent of laurel.

Here in the fork
　The brown nest is seated;
Four little blue eggs
　The mother keeps heated.

While we stand watching her
　Staring like gabies,
Safe in each egg are the
　Bird's little babies.

Soon the frail eggs they shall
　Chip, and upspringing
Make all the spring woods
　Merry with singing.

Younger than we are,
　O children, and frailer,
Soon in blue air they'll be,
　Singer and sailor.

We, so much older,
　Taller and stronger,
We shall look down on the
　Birdies no longer.

They shall go flying
　With musical speeches
High overhead in the
　Tops of the beeches.

In spite of our wisdom
　And sensible talking,
We on our feet must go
　Plodding and walking.

Wonderful Things

June Masters Bacher

A mother is all those
    wonderful things
The mind will never outgrow:
Walks in the woods to find
    things of spring;
How to cast angels in snow;

Warm chocolate smells when
    school is let out,
Ear tuned to hear every woe—
A mother is all those
    wonderful things
The mind will never outgrow.

A Mother's Heart

Alice B. Johnson

A mother's heart is tuned
   to listen for
The groping sound of hands
   upon the door—
The midnight striking of
   the mantel clock—

The turning of a key
   within the lock.
A mother knows
   when waiting hours are past
And each loved one
   is safely home at last.

To Mother

Jean Warren

A hushed
  and awesome silence
Comes in my heart today
As I think of all the things
  you've done:
The cheering words
  you've stopped to say,
The sweetness
  of your presence,
The courage in your smile,
The thoughts I know
  you gave to me,
And your prayers that
  ever go with me.
And I shall know
  that all through life
You'll stand by me,
  be ever near,
That through the storm,
  the stress, the strife
You'll be with me,
  my mother dear.

Mother Heart

Joy Belle Burgess

She fondly holds within her arms
Her little one, contented and asleep,
And finds within her mother-heart
Divine, sweet moments of peace.

The rocking chair so gently stirs
In rhythm with her humming,
While all her world, her joy and pride,
Lies cuddled in arms warm and loving.

She fondly holds his little hand
As he ventures forth to walk,
And oft repeats a simple word
As he desires to learn and talk.

When playtime brings a bruise, a tear,
Her tenderness meets every need,
And with each day, each passing year,
Her loving heart instructs and leads.

She fondly guides her growing son
As he matures, becomes a man,
And helps instill a deep-rooted faith,
High ideals, noble and grand;

And the love that ties her to her child
Is bestowed by God above,
For no human or earthly power can sever
The immortality of a mother's love.

Portrait

Marion Plunkett

There is an unseen strength within your being,
A wisdom, old as life and sure as death;
And in your eyes are thoughts
* beyond man's seeing,*
Steadfast as stones, soft as a firefly's breath.

Thoughts for the poor whose needs
* have been your care,*
For the distressed who say they cannot pray
But who have knelt with you in silent prayer
And risen with new faith to meet the day.

There's beauty in your lovely silver hair,
And on your lips a sweet, courageous smile;
Although of grief and pain
* you've had your share,*
Without complaint you traveled every mile.

* Enduring is the faith in God that lies*
* Within your soul and shines in your dear eyes.*

Photo Opposite
LILACS AND DECORATIVE JAR
D. Petku/H. Armstrong Roberts

Changeless

Katherine Edelman

The world is very beautiful,
Sky and land and sea;

The dawn, the glowing sunset,
With blossoms on a tree,

The singing stars, the moonbeam's glow,
A garden in the spring,

The gleam of silver on a lake,
A redbird on the wing.

But neither stretching skies of blue
Nor flower nor stars above

Holds quite as much of angel's touch
As mother's changeless love.

STRAWBERRY ANGEL FOOD CAKE

May is strawberry month. April's tiny white blossoms have weathered stubborn spring rains; suddenly, as if by magic, the beautiful crimson berries appear. But May is also the month to pay tribute to our mothers. This Mother's Day, why not celebrate with a delectable Strawberry Angel Food Cake? Easy to make, this recipe is the perfect light dessert for a spring day.

1	cup cake flour
1½	cups sugar
¼	teaspoon nutmeg
12	large egg whites
1¼	teaspoons cream of tartar
½	teaspoon salt
1	teaspoon vanilla
2	cups whipping cream
2	tablespoons powdered sugar
2	tablespoons cocoa
1	quart fresh strawberries, stemmed and halved

Preheat oven to 375°. Sift together flour, ½ cup sugar, and nutmeg. In mixing bowl, beat egg whites until frothy; add cream of tartar, salt, and vanilla. Beat until soft peaks form. Gradually beat in remaining sugar, 1 tablespoon at a time, until stiff, shiny peaks form. Fold in flour mixture. Spoon batter into ungreased 10 x 4-inch tube pan. Cut gently through batter to remove large air bubbles. Bake 30 minutes or until pick inserted into center of cake comes out clean. Invert cake on rack to cool.

Slice cake horizontally 1 inch from top; set aside top piece. To form a tunnel, make two circular cuts around inside of cake, 1 inch from outer edge and 1 inch from inner edge. Slice to within 1 inch of cake bottom. Gently pull out cake from within cuts; place hollowed cake on serving plate. In a bowl combine cream, sugar, and cocoa; whip just until stiff peaks form. Fold half the strawberries into half the whipped cream; spoon into cake, pressing down firmly. Replace cake top; press gently. Frost cake with remaining cream mixture. Arrange remaining strawberries on top of cake. Chill 15 minutes before slicing.

Makes 10 to 12 servings.

Recipe and photo courtesy California Strawberry Advisory Board

Country
CHRONICLE
——— Lansing Christman ———

We always referred to May as apple-blossom time in my childhood home in Upstate New York, more than eight hundred miles north of these Piedmont acres where I now live. Each spring I would walk through the orchards when the trees were in their heavy May bloom. The symphony of the honeybees as they probed the blossoms for one of their richest harvests of the year reminded me to pause and savor the sweetness of spring.

For the bees, and for me, there certainly would be more harvests to come. In the honey-

suckle vines along the road, in the clover fields, and in the profusion of summer flowers would be sight and scent and sound to fill long, sweet summer days and soft, warm evenings.

But spring reached for its fulfillment there in those orchards. Fresh and new and full of promise, May was not merely a prelude to the summer; it was a time to be treasured. The music of the honeybees lured me into the lacy white orchards, and there, I too made a harvest of the gifts of the fullness of spring.

I have held on to the lesson of those faraway honeybees. Today I still pause to find God's craftsmanship in all that I see and hear. And now that it is May again, although I am miles and years away from those New York apple orchards, I can still hear May's sweet symphony, as rhythmic as the purling waters in the rill and as tender as the chiming bells of the wood thrush's song.

The author of two published books, Lansing Christman has been contributing to Ideals *for almost twenty years. Mr. Christman has also been published in several American, foreign, and braille anthologies. He lives in rural South Carolina.*

IN BEAUTY

Vera Hardman

When the golden fingers of the sun
Draw draperies of the dawn,

Or when the silver moon at night
Glides like a graceful swan,

When the magic of the springtime
Makes flowers bloom anew,

Such beauty brings me thoughts of one
Who walked in beauty too.

Photo Opposite
FLOWERS FROM THE GARDEN
Comstock, Inc.

Mrs. Roosevelt's Plan

If boys are drafted, why not girls? Mrs. Roosevelt sees no reason why not. Since the beginning of the depression she has often discussed with the President a cherished plan: drafting U.S. girls for a year of compulsory service. Last week, like other citizens of the District of Columbia, Mrs. Roosevelt registered for voluntary civilian defense, and brought up again her plan for compulsory female training.

Compulsory as Mrs. Roosevelt's plan would be, it would not be drastic. The draft would be only an extension of the girls' compulsory education. Drafted girls between the ages of eighteen and twenty-four would be placed on the same footing as men, given the same subsistence, same wages. They would learn switchboard operation, nurses' aid, hospital work, buying and preparation of food, automobile driving, map reading, sewing, budgeting, as well as such mechanical skills as they wanted to learn. Most girls would put in their year at home, would leave home only if they wanted some sort of training which they could not get at home (and if their parents were willing to let them go away).

When the draft bill was being planned last year, Mrs. Roosevelt kept telephoning the President from her Val Kill cottage to urge that her draft-women program be included. If you are going to mobilize and train a nation, she argued, why leave out half the nation? But the President knew, and said, that no Congressman would touch a bill containing compulsory training for girls.

Two months ago, Mrs, Roosevelt brought up her plan in the *Ladies Home Journal*. It did not evoke overwhelming enthusiasm. In fact, most comment suggested that it scared the daylights out of U. S. men. Last week, after registering as a defense volunteer, Mrs. Roosevelt went to Manhattan, there, at Mayor LaGuardia's request, inspected prospective uniforms for volunteers, confessed to "a little confusion in thinking about uniforms before being entirely certain what work is to be done in them." In short, although no one in the Government, from the President down, supported her in it, she was still set on getting women in the draft.

Originally printed in *Time*, June 23, 1941.

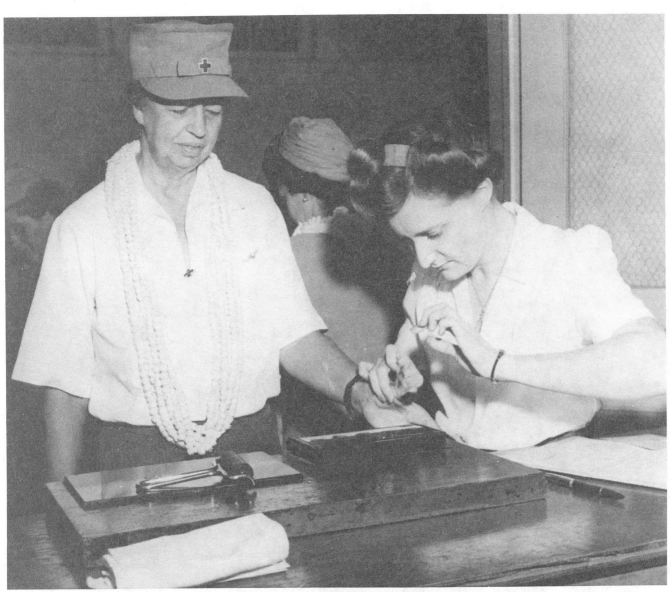

During a tour of Hawaii, Eleanor Roosevelt has her fingerprints taken for an Office of Civilian Defense identification card.
UPI/Bettmann Photos

Happy He with Such a Mother

Alfred, Lord Tennyson

I loved her: one
Not learned, save in gracious household ways,
Nor perfect, nay, but full of tender wants;
No angel, but a dearer being, all dipped
In angel instincts, breathing Paradise.
Interpreter between the gods and men,
Who looked all native in her place and yet
On tiptoe seemed to touch upon a sphere
Too gross to tread, and all male minds perforce
Swayed to her from the orbits as they moved
And girdled her with music. Happy he
With such a mother, faith in womankind
Beats within his blood and trusts all things high
Come easy to him; and though he trip and fall,
He shall not blind his soul with clay.

A Store-Bought Dress

Marion McGuire

I looked at the dark blue dress in the window of Malvena's Boutique every Wednesday of the summer of 1936. It was a formal made of a shiny material. It had a ruffled collar, little cap sleeves, a peplum, and an artificial rose at the waist. It cost $2.95.

I had never owned a store-bought dress before. My grandmother, a seamstress who lived in her sewing room surrounded by patterns, fabric, binding tape, spools of thread, pins, and needles, disapproved of ready-made clothes. "You meet yourself coming and going," she declared, kneeling before me to pin up a hem. But I was a restless seventeen-year-old, and I was envious of friends who did not wear homemade dresses. I dreamed of the day when I would be rich enough to walk into Malvena's Boutique as a customer.

I visited the store weekly as part of my summer job as an unpaid reporter for the local newspaper. My beat was the north side of Gardena Boulevard, from the Boutique, past Ernie's Ice Cream Shoppe, to Robertson's Hardware. Another reporter covered the opposite side of the street. We would walk into the businesses and inquire if any newsworthy events had gone on during the past week. Then we walked back to the office and typed our stories.

This pleasant life went on for five weeks. Then Mr. Guild, the editor, promoted me. The other reporter had a week off. "You do the whole job," Mr. Guild said, "and I'll pay you ten dollars."

This astonished my grandmother. "You can save it for college," she said. But I had other plans. When I went into the boutique for my usual interview, I tried on the blue dress. It seemed perfect. I had never worn that shade of blue before and when I looked at my face in the mirror I saw a beautiful stranger. I asked Malvena to put the dress in the back room and promised to come back with the money as soon as I'd been paid.

I had no idea I was making a mistake until I opened the box at home and saw Grandmother's face. She was offended. "Why would you want this thing?" she demanded, pinching the thin material. "And for $2.95? I could make two decent dresses for that kind of money." She closed the sewing machine, cleared the pattern books from her bed, and went to sit by the window. My grandmother loved to make clothes for the child I had been; I had made her feel unappreciated.

I put the dress in my closet and did not mention it again. My summer job ended, the school year began, and I entered college.

There was a formal dance for freshmen that fall, and I told my grandmother of my plans to go. "You could wear your prom dress," she said. "It's only been worn once."

Grandmother had made my prom dress. It was a beautiful white organdy, with puffed sleeves and a full skirt. But I was no longer the same child who went to the prom. I was a college student—practically grown-up. I chose to wear the store-bought dress.

On the night of the formal, the college gym was decorated with balloons and crepe paper streamers, and there was a live band. I felt totally sophisticated. My dress swished delightfully around my ankles. The small cloud of guilt caused by Grandmother's disappointment soon vanished.

And then I saw the other girl. She was a short, pink-cheeked blond, curved in many places. She was wearing my dress. The dark blue matched her eyes and the rose at her waist nestled perfectly to her side. The dress looked as if it had been made especially for her.

I tried to steer away, but my partner, oblivious to the problem, followed the other girl across the dance floor. When the music finally stopped, I made such a swift move for a chair that my heel caught in my skirt and twisted my ankle.

"I think it's broken," I gasped, and that ended the evening.

Grandmother was waiting up. When she saw my swollen ankle she ran some water into the tub. "Take off that dress," she said, "and start soaking your foot."

Sitting on the edge of the tub with my foot in the water, I told her about the other girl.

"Well, that happens with store-bought things," she said, serenely. "You meet yourself coming and going."

The next morning I awoke to the whir of the sewing machine. My grandmother was busy making my college wardrobe. She was whistling softly.

CRAFTWORKS

Decorative Wallpaper Fan

Growing up in rural Tennessee, Shirley Jones learned never to throw anything away. Today, she puts this lesson to good use, making these lovely fans from leftover wallpaper, silk flowers and ribbons from old corsages, spare pieces of lace, and whatever else she has on hand. The directions below are for the fan pictured opposite, but with the basic method and your own creative instincts, endless variations are possible.

MATERIALS NEEDED:

1	20 by 30-inch piece of wallpaper
3½	yards 2½-inch paisley ribbon
3½	yards 2-inch lace ribbon
2	yards 1⅜-inch paisley ribbon
2	yards 1⅜-inch lace ribbon
1½	yards 1-inch solid color ribbon
1½	yards 1-inch lace ribbon
1	yard ¼-inch solid color cord
1	string artificial pearls
6	large silk flowers with stems
1	spray small silk flowers
1	bunch small dried flowers
10	small silk roses
	Floral wire; hole punch; hot glue gun and glue sticks; transparent tape; clothespins

MAKING FAN

Cut two 31-inch strips each of 2½-inch paisley and 2-inch lace ribbon. Hot glue one strip of paisley ribbon ¼ inch from edge along both 30-inch sides of wallpaper, leaving ½-inch overlap on each end and keeping right sides up. Glue lace ribbon directly on top of paisley. Set aside to dry 5 minutes.

Starting at one of the 20-inch edges, fold wallpaper accordion style into 1-inch pleats. Hold each pleat securely, being careful not to puncture paper. Use clothespins to secure pleats while folding.

After pleating is complete, fold the accordion in half to form fan, aligning ribbon borders at top. With right sides facing, hot glue center pleats of fan, pinching tightly to hold in place while glue sets. Let dry 5 minutes.

Keeping bordered edges even, make a handle by pinching together the fan in center 1 inch from bottom. Secure handle with transparent tape.

Punch holes in center of each pleat ½ inch from lower border edge. Thread the cord through holes; glue ends to back of fan. Set aside to dry 10 minutes.

MAKING BOW

Place remaining 2-inch lace on top of 2½-inch paisley ribbon. Keeping lace side up, make a loop 1 inch in diameter on one end. Pinching with thumb and forefinger, twist once and make a loop using 10 inches of ribbon. Repeat for three more loops of equal size, holding all loops together between thumb and forefinger, and twisting before each loop. For streamers, make one last loop of remaining 20 inches. Attach all loops with floral wire; pull tight to secure. Cut last and longest loop in half for streamers.

Repeat with 1⅜-inch paisley ribbon and 1⅜-inch lace, tying five loops of 9½ inches each.

Repeat with 1-inch ribbon and 1-inch lace, tying four loops of 7½ inches each.

Attach the small flowers to streamers. Place smallest bow on top of medium bow and attach with floral wire. Secure both to large bow to create one large bow. String pearls through center of bow; attach with wire.

DECORATING FAN

Position bow in center of fan; secure with generous amounts of hot glue. Maintain pressure against fan until glue sets. Following the placement pictured opposite, arrange flowers behind bow and glue to fan. When fan is dry, punch hole in the back of center pleat about ½ inch from top. Thread cord or wire through hole; hang on wall or door.

Shirley Jones lives in Lafayette, Tennessee, with her husband and three children.

COLLECTOR'S CORNER

Victorian Lace

Karen S. Hodge

Young Victorian woman in lace-trimmed dress.   The Bettmann Archive

Chances are that if you have pieces of old lace left in your attic or tucked away in a cedar-lined trunk, it is Victorian era lace. That is, it was made, either by hand or by machine, between 1837 to 1901, when Queen Victoria ruled England.

Even before Victoria, many English queens were partial to lace. Mary II, wife of William of Orange, was an avid and skilled lace maker. Queen Anne used lace lavishly for her wardrobe and for decoration. Queen Charlotte, wife of George III, always wore lace at court.

But it was during Queen Victoria's long reign that lace enjoyed its greatest popularity. Fashion during Victoria's reign saw great changes; but throughout the era, women's apparel continued to be heavily trimmed with great quantities of beautiful, intricately designed lace.

At her death, Victoria's collection of lace was valued at approximately seventy-six thousand dollars. Much of her personal collection can be seen at the Victoria and Albert Museum in London. Her wedding dress of white satin trimmed with Honiton bobbin lace is on display at the London Museum.

You need not be descended from royalty, however, to have in your possession valuable lace collectibles. Lace is one of the few antiques that is under-valued and cannot be faked. Determining the age of a piece of lace requires experience, and it is not an exact science. But it is safe to assume that only rarely is lace from a family collection much over one hundred years old. Possible exceptions to this rule are bridal gowns and veils, and christening robes which have been carefully stored between uses.

Queen Victoria in one of her many lace veils.   The Bettmann Archive

lace-making was included with embroidery, crochet, and tatting as a favorite pastime for ladies. But industrial advances in the early nineteenth century led to machine-made lace which so skillfully reproduced the old patterns that it is now hard to tell the machine lace from the handmade.

Condition, design, rarity, and workmanship are the basics which determine the intrinsic value of old lace. Still, some pieces are valued for sentimental reasons more than for these objective factors.

Lace lovers who want to know how to clean and preserve lace pieces will find several books on the subject. There are also magazines devoted exclusively to the subject of Victorian collectibles. Both can provide ideas and inspiration for refurbishing and displaying prized Victorian lace pieces.

A damaged wedding veil that cannot be restored may find new life as a christening gown. Collars and cuffs once worn by your great grandmother might complete a new dress. A bit of period lace may be just the thing to set off a framed wedding invitation or a period photograph.

So if you have inherited a bag of old lace, or if you have accumulated bits and pieces over the years, remember that while some of it was made for the dime-store and some might be museum quality, beauty is in the eye of the collector, and there is nothing quite as feminine, romantic, or whimsical as lace. It is one of the first images brought to mind by the term "Victorian."

Karen Hodge writes articles, essays, and educational materials from her home in Antioch, Tennessee.

Looking at books with illustrations on period costumes can help you date certain pieces. For instance, early in the era small, apron-shaped or semi-circular veils were worn. The mid-Victorian period saw shoulder flounces—called "berthas"—and full lace undersleeves as the height of fashion. Lace was favored for evening wear throughout the period.

Handmade lace was never produced in quantity in the United States. In Europe during the 1800s, however, lace was so in favor that

Visiting Grandma

Oh, how I loved to visit Grandma
In my childhood days.
She was the idol of my life
In so many ways.

I loved so much to watch her knit;
On a stool by her feet
I'd serenely sit
As she patiently tried
To teach me what to do.

We'd sing together, she and I.
I'd grow so sleepy by and by
Then on her lap she'd cuddle me;
Soon, I'd be napping happily.

At three in the afternoon
Cookies there'd be,
With tea for Grandma
And milk for me.

When nighttime came
Off to bed I'd go
And nestle 'neath covers
As white as snow.

When I would waken
How happy I'd be;
Ready for more
Of Grandma's hospitality.

Lucille Simmons
Columbus, Ohio

Reflections

My Grandma

Watching Grandma from the window
Standing by her flower bed
I must wonder what she is thinking
As she plucks a rose of red.

She is singing softly to herself
Slowly walking to and fro
With a somber face expression
A sweet smile begins to show.

Watching nature from her standpoint
As she sits down in her chair
The wind doth blow so gently
Through her long and gray white hair.

She's my grandma, a gem she is
A place of love, divine and true.
This whole world would be so lonely
Without grandmas sweet like you.

Leon Burkholder
Milford, Indiana

Grandmother's Face

Like some rare bit of Persian lace
Or cracked glaze on Dresden plate,
The etchings on my grandmother's face
Were not thrown there by chance or fate;
Years wrought this artistry with care,
Recording every thought and deed;
The story of her life is there
Upon her face for all to read.

Vivian Buchan
Iowa City, Iowa

Editor's Note: Readers are invited to submit unpublished, original poetry, short anecdotes, and humorous reflections on life for possible publication in future *Ideals* issues. Please send copies only; manuscripts will not be returned. Writers receive $10 for each published submission. Send material to: "Readers' Reflections," Ideals Publishing Corporation, P.O. Box 140300, Nashville, TN 37214-0300.

TRAVELER'S Diary

Arch Rock, a beautiful limestone formation overlooking Lake Huron.

Mackinac Island

Mackinac Island, which lies in the cold waters of the Straits of Mackinac between Lake Michigan and Lake Huron, has been attracting travelers for thousands of years. Well before Europeans discovered the island, the Huron indians came to the area, drawn by the rich fishing in the surrounding lakes and bays. They named the region *Michilimackinac*, or "Land of the Great Turtle."

Since the days when the Hurons roamed the island's bays and shores, Mackinac has been a center for the French fur trade, a British military base, an American revolutionary fort, a resort for wealthy Victorians, and, finally, a national park. Through it all, Mackinac Island has retained a unique allure.

Today, the island continues to attract travelers with its commitment to providing a memorable vacation firmly rooted in its rich and color-ful heritage. No automobiles are allowed on Mackinac; transportation is by horse-drawn carriage, bicycle, or on foot. Nor do bridges or tunnels link Mackinac to the mainland; only the ferry brings visitors back and forth from Michigan. This isolation enhances a feeling of timelessness on the island and contributes to what has been called the "elegant laziness" of a vacation on Mackinac.

The first European to set foot on Mackinac Island was most likely Frenchman Jean Nicolet, who accidentally came upon the island in 1634 while searching for the route to China. Needless to say, China eluded Nicolet, but he took back to France wonderful tales of the region and its bounty. By 1660, French fur traders, inspired by Nicolet's tales, had established a small trading village on the northern side of the Straits. The French built Fort Michilimackinac on the southern shores of the straits to protect their growing fur trade.

French control of the region, however, did not last. After the French and Indian War, the British assumed control of Michilimackinac. During the American Revolution, the British moved the fort to the more defensible cliffs of Mackinac Island. A village grew on the shores of the bay below the fort, centered around St. Anne's church, which was moved there from the mainland and still stands today.

The majestic Grand Hotel, a Mackinac landmark for more than a century.

But British control was as short-lived as the French; following the American victory in the Revolution, the Straits of Mackinac came into American hands.

The Fort was to change hands once more, in the War of 1812, but eventually, the entire Michilimackinac region became a part of the new American nation. As peace and stability returned, the fur trade again prospered; and a new era in the history of the island began when John Jacob Astor, America's first millionaire, located his fur company headquarters on Mackinac Island.

By the mid-1830s, the fur trade had declined, but Astor's precedent had established a fashionable new destination for the nation's wealthy, who came to Mackinac to build summer homes. By the 1880s, elaborate Victorian cottages lined the shores of the island, and tourism overtook both fishing and the fur trade as the main commerce of the region. The cottages remain today, lending a wonderful Victorian flavor to Mackinac. The label "cottage," however, is somewhat misleading. Some of the structures are four stories high, with twelve to fifteen bedrooms, separate servant's quarters, and lush gardens.

Another remnant of the island's Victorian resort days is the Grand Hotel. Nowhere is the "elegant laziness" of Mackinac more pronounced than at the Grand, which is truly the visual centerpiece of the island. Built at the height of the island's resort era, the Grand Hotel boasts the longest porch of any hotel in the world and is the length of two football fields.

In 1875, Mackinac underwent its final transformation as it was named a United States National Park. (The park was later transferred to the state of Michigan.) Today, Mackinac Island State Park is a paradise for bicyclists and hikers. The shoreline creates an ideal eight mile loop around the island, and the hike through the middle of the island—"across the turtle's back"—is a pleasing three miles. Prehistoric limestone formations and the spectacular Arch Rock, a natural arch fifty feet across and one hundred feet above the water, combine with breathtaking views of the bays and Straits to create a striking landscape.

Mackinac is "open" year round, but the tourist season runs from mid-May through mid-October, and the best times to visit the island are spring and autumn. Lying elegantly in the waters of the Straits, Mackinac today is as alluring as ever, thanks to the beauty of its architecture, the magnificence of its natural setting, and the well-preserved heritage of all those who have called the island home.

Victorian cottages along Mackinac Island's West Bluff.

Photo Overleaf
MT. RANIER, WASHINGTON
Dick Dietrich Photography

Louisa May Alcott

In 1850, Louisa May Alcott was eighteen years old and a teacher in a Boston grammar school. Although she would one day create some of America's most cherished literature for children, Louisa was at this time still barely beyond her own childhood. But in a diary entry from that year, she wrote of her mother with a maturity and responsibility beyond her years:

I often think of what a hard life she has had since she married . . . so different from her early, easy days, the youngest and most petted of the family. I think she is a very brave, good woman; and my dream is to have a lovely, quiet home for her, with no debts or trouble to burden her.

At an age when most young women dream of their future independence, Louisa Alcott's dream was to provide comfort and security for her mother.

Abba Alcott, mother of Louisa and three other girls, had earned her daughter's devotion. In the often unstable world of Alcott family life,

Abba had been a constant, unshakable center. Bronson Alcott, Louisa's father, was a remarkable man and a loving, if unconventional, father. His career was devoted mainly to education, and he was an innovator in the field. The Alcott children were beneficiaries of these innovations, receiving instruction far beyond the norm for girls of their day. Louisa Alcott and her sisters grew up in a world where creativity and individuality were encouraged and cherished, and where Ralph Waldo Emerson and Henry David Thoreau were frequent house guests.

The other side of Bronson Alcott's influence upon the youth of his children, however, was less ideal. For along with his brilliance came instability and impracticality. His career was as full of disappointment as it was success. The Alcott children may have been always respected and well instructed, but they were frequently ill-fed and often made to deal with the adult pressures of poverty and deprivation.

In this world of change and contradiction, Abba Alcott was a constant, dependable presence. A woman of incredible stamina, she saw to the day to day care of her children and comforted them during the frequent absences and fluctuating fortunes of their father. Unlike Bronson, who perhaps in his zeal for educational innovation often looked upon his four girls as students rather than children, Abba never lost sight of the fact that her four girls needed the shelter and protection of a safe and steady home environment. She was willing to do whatever was necessary to provide for that need. Mrs. Alcott was an educated woman from a prominent Boston family with many material advantages. But, nonetheless, she was not above accepting menial labor to support her children, nor was she unwilling to go without so that they might not.

Abba was not simply a caretaker to her girls; she was an inspiration. In the eighteen-year-old mind of Louisa, her mother's life was full of sacrifice and hardship, and she set herself early to the task of relieving that hardship by easing the family's financial burden. Teaching was only one of many jobs that Louisa took on in her young adult life. At various times she worked as a governess, a companion, a seamstress, and a domes-tic servant, always driven by the goal of earning enough to ease her mother's load.

Success came to Louisa, finally, through her writing. With her novels and stories for children, Louisa created a new, eager audience of young readers who clamored for her books and brought to their author the long sought-after means of providing for her mother.

But something had happened, along the road to success, to Louisa's understanding of her mother's sacrifice. In the inscription to *Work*, Louisa May Alcott, as a grown woman, echoes the thoughts of the eighteen-year-old school teacher so intent upon providing comfort to her mother. But she also reveals a more mature understanding of the nature of that comfort. "*To My Mother*," she writes, "*whose life has been a long labor of love, this book is gratefully inscribed by her daughter*." What had been merely labor in the mind of the child was, to the woman, a loving, willing labor.

How had Louisa—a woman who never had a child of her own—come to understand so well the motivations of her mother? Perhaps the answer is to be found in her novels. Louisa's fictional worlds were made up, in large part, of characters and experiences from her own life. As she wrote—at first merely as a means of earning income—she delved into her own childhood for inspiration. What came back to her were not the moments of hardship and sacrifice, but the figure of a strong, nurturing mother and the world that she created for her family. Mrs. Alcott reappears in her daughter's *Little Women* as Mrs. March, providing the nurturing environment in which her four girls learn and grow. Her image, in fact, dominates nearly all of Louisa's stories for children. Mother and home became the foundation for Louisa's novels as she came to realize that they had been the anchor in her own life.

And this, after all, is a greater tribute to Abba Alcott than any sum of money. With *Little Women* and countless other stories, Louisa May Alcott taught generations of young readers what her mother had known all along, that it is in the quiet security of the domestic sphere that children learn life's greatest lessons.

Her Voice

Laura Hope Wood

I stand and wait
To hear a sound so sweet
　across the miles
That stills my racing heart,
And I am left serene
　and calm,
So reassured of love
　and satisfied.
No other sound can ever
　mean the same.
For when I am old and
　sands of time are low,
It will reverberate
　within my heart,
And I will know,
There is no greater joy
　or sweeter melody
Compared with when
　mother's voice
Rings clear
　and answers me.

WILD ROSES AT MONTAUK BEACH
Long Island, New York
Ed Cooper Photography

A Grandmother's Gifts

We've recently come from a visit with my parents, and this Mother's Day, I have a whole new appreciation for my mother—as a grandmother. She has always been a good mother, but she really outdoes herself as a grandparent! I've watched her develop this role over the years as our three children have come along, and I must admit that she has mastered this gentle art of "grandmothering."

Grandmothers are very special people. As all

children know, their sole purpose is to make life more delightful and interesting. I remember my own grandmother doing this for me. She was willing to do all sorts of ridiculous things my mother didn't have time for. One afternoon, Grandma and I turned the entire Sunday paper into a flotilla of paper boats—hundreds of them. And on another occasion, she and I sat out under the black walnut tree staring at the sky. We made up stories about the clouds as they passed overhead, pushed along by a summer wind. I recalled this as I watched my mother stretched out flat on her back in the waist-high grass, my son nestled next to her hiding from his big brother. "Shhhh," she whispered conspiratorially, and he looked at her with awe-filled eyes, amazed and delighted that a real-live grown-up would play this game with him.

Grandmas also have access to wonderful treasures, and they are never too selfish to share them. And grandmothers rarely say "Don't touch." My Grandma had a tiny gold locket on a chain that Grandpa had given her when they were young. She would let me wear it now and then and, when I was ten years old, she gave it to me to keep. I can still feel the wonder of it. And I recalled that wonder once again when I saw my daughter gasp with delight as my mother opened a box of costume jewelry and let her granddaughter rummage through it. She spent hours sorting "diamonds" and "rubies" and "emeralds" like a pirate princess. Then, when Grandma wrapped her in an old feather boa and draped her with gems, I laughed out loud as I recognized the look of adoration in my daughter's eyes.

Grandmas also have treasures of other kinds. They know all the best stories about when mommies and daddies were small. I can remember begging my grandmother to tell me about my father when he was a little boy, hardly believing that the man I adored had ever been a child like me. And she would dramatically relate the times when he had been naughty and chased the chickens with a broom, and the terrible time when his finger had been cut with an axe. It was a key to a secret well of information about my favorite hero, and I never tired of hearing the stories. This too is a grandmotherly art, I find, as I listen to my mother tell of my youthful misadventures to my eager offspring! It is a generational fairy tale wherein children begin to understand that their parents once were young and vulnerable too.

Grandmothers have a knack, as well, for teaching lessons in the most delightful ways. I baked my first cookies at Grandma's house. They weren't the best I ever made, but they were sure the most interesting. Before coming to America as a young bride, Grandma had been a cook in an English household. She cooked everything by hand—a handful of sugar, three handfuls of flour, a pinch of salt. I mixed and squished and rolled and pounded, all with my bare hands, savoring the textures and the making, if not the end results.

Last summer I thought of Grandma's lessons as my mother took her granddaughter by the hand and led her to a little patch of ground in the corner of the backyard. Months earlier she had planted potatoes there and now their dark green leaves nodded in the late summer sun. Mother invited my city-bred daughter to pull the plants from the loosened earth, and I watched as she tugged them free, squealing with childish delight at the tiny red potatoes dangling from the hairy roots. She scrubbed them with muddy fingers, placed them tenderly in the steamer, then beamed with pride as we enjoyed them that night for supper. That day my daughter learned about seeds and soil and sun and how they are all wrapped together in the mysterious cycle of life. These lessons of her first "harvest" at her Grandma's side will not be easily forgotten.

As I watched it all I was reminded of life's never-ending cycles. How daughters become mothers and mothers turn into grandmothers and children are enriched by knowing that families do not end.

Pamela Kennedy is a freelance writer of short stories, articles, essays, and children's books. Married to a naval officer and the mother of three children, she has made her home on both U.S. coasts and currently resides in Hawaii. She draws her material from her own experiences and memories, adding bits of imagination to create a story or mood.

OLD MOTHERS

Grace Noll Crowell

They draw me to them: women who have grown
Wise with the wisdom that right living brings.
Old mothers who have suffered and have known
A triumph over many conquered things,
Who have grown gentle, trusting day by day,
Who have grown patient, serving through the years;
Who, having prayed much, have learned how to pray,
And weeping—learned how futile were their tears.

They wear such certainty within their eyes:
A sureness that no questioning can shake;
All is so clear to them—they are so wise,
The way was made so plain that they should take.
If one should come to them—his faith grown dim—
Their faith would light the fires anew in him.

Photo Opposite
ROSES AND BABY'S BREATH
Ulrike Schneiders/H. Armstrong Roberts

I Do Not Walk Alone

Goldie Capers Smith

My mother walked by night, and where she passed,
Contentment spread, and safety, for her hand
Brought magic to a pillow. She would stand
Before a window, making shutters fast
Against a midnight storm, her love a shield
No javelin of light could force to yield.

Safe in her presence, certain she would keep
All evil out, I gave myself to sleep.
Now as I walk from room to room by night
Smoothing the covers over a restless child,
Or closing shutters when the night is wild,
To keep at bay the storm's unearthly light,
A quiet step accompanies my own,
And in the dark I do not walk alone.

Readers' Forum

What an amazing and most pleasant surprise! In the Home edition of Ideals, *on the 50 years Ago page was a photo of nurses knitting during World War I. What would the odds be that one of the nurses in that group would see the photo?*

We were in the 10th Evacuation Hospital and as I recall, the photo was taken at a camp near Brisbane, Australia. Australia had lovely wool yarn and some of the Australian women taught us how to knit.

I am the nurse in the center of the photo. The nurse on the right died a few years ago. The nurse on the left is Muriel Harley Rickwood and resides in Brookfield, Massachusetts. I'm Elise Pooler Lambert, and I live in Orrington, Maine. I shall show the photo to all of my friends.

Elise C. Lambert
Orrington, Maine

I wish to express my happiness with your article on Legendary Americans which was Jane Addams in Ideals Friendship. *My home is near the area of Jane Addams childhood days. I have always been proud of the work done by Jane Addams in Hull House. Thank you for including her in* Ideals Friendship.

Gladys Geist
Davis, Illinois

Many years ago I received my first copy of Ideals *from a customer of mine. The issue was included in my wedding gift from her. The* Ideals *was Sweetheart 1954. I still have this issue along with my many other older issues. The lady who gave me my first copy was Georgia Moore Eberling, who so loved your publications. You did publish some of her poems. . . . I have had a subscription to your magazine for many years and have enjoyed them all! It really pleased me last week when your Friendship* Ideals *arrived and on page 69 I found one of Mrs. Eberling's poems. Thank you for all the happiness you have given to so many of us because of your beautiful publications.*

Laura Jamnick
Pueblo, Colorado

Editor's Note: "Thoughts of a Busy Mother," the poem that appears on page 22 of this issue, was also published in last year's Mother's Day issue. Unfortunately, last year we attributed the poem to Margaret D. Nanny. Since then we have learned that the author is actually Katherine Cahill of Pine Plains, New York. We apologize to Ms. Cahill for our error.

* * *

ideals
Celebrating Life's Most Treasured Moments